2025 SOCIAL MEDIA CONTENT PLANNER & GUIDE

With CHATGPT TIPS & AI PROMPTS

Guaranteed better results in less time

Louise McDonnell

Published by Orla Kelly Publishing.

Hi there!

Thank you for choosing my planner! My goal is to empower you to consistently create top-notch social media content, whether it's for your regular posts or paid promotions. With over a decade of experience helping businesses and nonprofits thrive online, I've fine-tuned my approach for 2025 to make sure you're always ahead of the curve.

At SellOnSocial.Media, my team and I continue to manage successful social media campaigns for businesses, and through the Academy, I'm still dedicated to showing you the exact steps needed to get measurable results. This planner reflects the latest trends and strategies, so you can deliver high-quality content week after week, perfectly aligned with your business goals.

Visit www.SellOnSocialMedia.Academy/2025Resources to access all the updated prompts (including key dates) in the 2025 Social Media Prompts and Content Planning Calendar Template. You are also invited to attend a live masterclass on **ChatGPT-Powered Content Strategy: Planning 2025's Social Media Success** taking place on January 22nd, at 11 am ET / 4 pm GMT. In this interactive session, Louise will guide you through setting up a powerful content strategy for 2025 using ChatGPT prompts to brainstorm ideas, plan effective campaigns, and align your social media efforts with your business goals.

Let's stay connected on social media! You can find me at @sellonsocialm across all platforms. You can also connect with me on LinkedIn under Louise McDonnell. If you share photos of this year's planner, don't forget to tag me and use the hashtag #Kickstart2025.

Once again, thank you for choosing my planner. I'm thrilled to be part of your 2025 social media journey!

To your success,

Louise McDonnell
www.SellOnSocialMedia.Academy/2025Resources

Personal Details

Name:

Address:

Email:

In case of emergency please contact

Name:

Address:

Telephone:

Mobile:

Passwords

Brand Colours

Company Registration Number

Tax Reference Number

Vat Number

Tax Clearance Reference

Notes

CONTENTS

FREE SOCIAL MEDIA RESOURCES

Visit **www.SellOnSocialMedia.Academy/2025Resources** where you can download the following free tools.

2025 Social Media Online Content Planning Calendar
(Value $159)

This 12-month content calendar is designed to help you and your team organize and coordinate social media content with ease. It's a complete planning tool to keep your social strategy on track all year. Inside, you'll also find over 400 prompts from this book, giving you fresh ideas and engaging content—perfect for staying organized, on-brand, and consistently inspired.

www.SellOnSocialMedia.Academy/2025Resources

Claim $377 of free online resources at www.SellOnSocialMedia.Academy/2025Resources

↘

LIVE TRAINING

ChatGPT-Powered Content Strategy: Planning 2025's Social Media Success

(Value $218)

Join Louise McDonnell for a one-hour live training session on **Wednesday, January 22nd, at 11 am ET /4 pm GMT**.

In this interactive session, Louise will guide you through setting up a powerful content strategy for 2025 using ChatGPT prompts to brainstorm ideas, plan effective campaigns, and align your social media efforts with your business goals. Plus, you'll have the chance to ask questions and gain insights in real time.

Can't make it live? Don't worry—playback will be available afterward so you can revisit the session anytime in 2025.

HARNESSING THE POWER OF SOCIAL MEDIA IN A SMARTPHONE-DRIVEN WORLD

The internet has become part of our daily lives. Think about how much time you spend on your phone—your potential customers are doing the same. A report from April 2023 shows that 5.18 billion people, or 64.6% of the global population, are internet users, and 4.8 billion, or 59.9%, are active on social media.

With smartphones always close by, this is a unique chance for businesses to connect with their audience. But just having a social media profile isn't enough; to make the most of it, businesses need to follow key principles.

- **Consistency**: In the ever-evolving world of social media, consistency is key. Regularly showing up on your chosen platforms keeps your brand fresh in the minds of your audience.
- **Authenticity**: Authenticity builds trust. Share your genuine voice, values, and stories. Authentic content resonates with your audience on a deeper level.
- **Be Real**: Share images, videos, and content featuring you and your team. Faceless, generic social media accounts simply don't work.
- **Engagement**: Being present isn't enough; engage actively with your audience. Respond to comments, answer questions, and create dialogues to strengthen connections.
- **Targeting**: Know your ideal customer and their social media habits. Tailor your content to reach them where they hang out online.

ESTABLISHING YOUR BRAND VOICE: INTERACTIVE WORKBOOK

Having a compelling brand story is key to standing out and connecting with your audience. Your brand narrative tells potential customers who you are, what you stand for, and why they should choose you. A strong story helps build trust, loyalty, and long-lasting relationships.

This workbook is here to help you create a narrative that truly reflects your brand's purpose and values while resonating deeply with your audience. Use the prompts and exercises to guide you step by step.

Workbook Overview: How to Use This Tool

1. **Reflect**: Take some time to think through each section. Use the space provided to jot down your thoughts, and don't worry about getting it perfect on the first try—refine as you go.
2. **Document**: Write down your brand's core messages. These will be the foundation of your brand story and messaging strategy.
3. **Refine**: Come back to this workbook from time to time to make sure your narrative evolves along with your business.

What Is Your Mission Statement?
Your mission statement is at the heart of your brand story. It defines your purpose and guides everything you do.

Prompt: Write a clear, concise mission statement that answers:
- What is your brand's purpose?
- What values guide your business?

Who is your Ideal Customer?

Knowing who you're speaking to is crucial for shaping your narrative. Define your ideal audience—who they are, what they care about, and what challenges they face.

Prompt: Who is your ideal customer? What are their pain points, frustrations, and desires?

What Results and Benefits Do You Provide?

Customers want to know how your product or service will make their lives better. Focus on the results you achieve and what sets you apart from competitors.

Prompt: How does your product/service transform your customers' lives? What are five specific benefits that set you apart?

What are your core values?

Your core values guide every decision you make and should be reflected in everything from branding to customer service.

Prompt: List 3-5 core values that define your business. How do these values shape your daily operations and decisions?

Brand personality and tone

Your brand's personality and tone shape how you communicate with your audience. They determine how your customers perceive and relate to you.

Exercise: Choose 3-5 personality traits that describe your brand, and define the tone of voice that aligns with these traits.

- **Personality**: Friendly, trustworthy, innovative
- **Tone of Voice**: Casual, approachable, and conversational

What are your brand's goals and aspirations?
Setting clear goals helps guide your brand's direction and growth.

Prompt: What are your short-term and long-term goals? Where do you envision your brand in the next 5 years?

Emotions and tone
Emotions are powerful in helping customers connect with your brand. Defining the emotions you want to evoke will help shape your tone and messaging.

Prompt: What emotions do you want your brand to evoke? How does your tone support these emotions? Do you want to inspire, comfort, or energize your audience?

What is your elevator pitch?

An elevator pitch is a concise statement that sums up your brand's story and value proposition. It should be short, impactful, and memorable.

Exercise: Craft an elevator pitch that summarizes your brand's purpose, what you offer, and why customers should choose you.

Describe your brand in three words

Distill your brand's essence into just three defining words. These should capture the core of who you are and how you want to be seen.

Use this workbook as a living document. As your business grows, revisit these questions to refine your narrative and keep your story aligned with your goals. A clear, compelling brand story not only sets you apart from the competition but also fosters lasting connections with your audience.

PLANNING SOCIAL MEDIA CONTENT

Planning your social media content is so important to make sure your posts align with your business goals and really connect with your audience. Unlike traditional marketing, where you can plan everything months in advance, social media needs a bit more flexibility. I actually recommend not planning too far ahead—doing so can lead to posts that lack relevance or creativity.

Here's how to plan your social media content effectively while keeping it flexible and high-quality:

1. **Align Your Social Media with Your Marketing Campaigns**: Make sure your social media content supports your larger marketing campaigns. Whether you're launching a new product, running a seasonal promotion, or hosting an event, your social media should amplify these efforts. By aligning your content with your campaigns, you create consistency across all channels and make a bigger impact.

   TOP TIP: Use a content calendar to schedule posts around major campaign dates, focusing on key promotions or product launches.

2. **Get in the Habit of Planning Regularly**: Instead of planning weeks or months in advance, try spending some time each week or every couple of weeks to plan and tweak your social media posts. This way, your content stays fresh, relevant, and responsive to any trends or changes that come up.

   ACTION STEP: Set aside time at the start of each week to outline your social media content, and make sure to include any new developments or trends from the past week.

3. **Use Prompts for Inspiration**: If you ever feel stuck for ideas, turn to the prompts in this guide. They're great for sparking creativity and adding variety to your posts. (You can find these prompts in the content planning calendar available in the free resources that come with this guide: https:// www.SellOnSocialMedia. Academy/2025Resources).

   TOP TIP: When using prompts, don't just post for the sake of it. Make sure each post ties back to your core business messages and goals so that everything has a purpose and supports your brand story.

4. **Create unique, authentic posts**: One common mistake is posting generic content that doesn't really connect with your audience. Instead, focus on creating unique, engaging posts that reflect your brand's personality and values. Tailored, visually appealing content that offers real value is much more likely to generate engagement. **AVOID**: Copy-pasting content from other platforms or sources. Make sure each post is tailored to your brand's voice.

5. **Use paid reach to boost your visibility**: Organic reach is great, but social media algorithms can make it hard for unpaid posts to be seen. To reach more people, consider using paid reach to boost key posts, especially those tied to major campaigns or important content. Paid reach lets you target specific audiences, making sure your message gets in front of the right people. **TOP TIP**: Allocate part of your budget to promote posts that are already performing well or that align with your sales goals.

6. **Review and adjust continuously**: Social media success isn't just about posting content—it's also about monitoring how it performs and making changes as needed. Regularly review your posts and campaigns to see what's working and what isn't. If certain types of content aren't resonating with your audience, tweak your approach. Flexibility is the key to keeping your social media presence successful. **ACTION STEP**: At the end of each week, take a look at what worked well and what didn't. Use that information to guide your content plan for the next week.

PLATFORM POPULARITY IN 2025: CHOOSING THE RIGHT SOCIAL MEDIA FOR YOUR BUSINESS AND AUDIENCE

In today's digital landscape, selecting the right social media platform is key to reaching and engaging your audience. Each platform offers unique features and targets specific demographics, so it's important to understand where your audience spends their time. Here's a quick overview of the most popular platforms in 2025 and how your business can make the most of them:

1. **Facebook**: If you're looking to reach a wide, diverse audience, Facebook is still where it's at. With 3.07 billion monthly active users, it's particularly strong among 25-34-year-olds. While younger users may be shifting to TikTok and Instagram, Facebook is perfect for engaging older millennials, Gen X, and building a sense of community.
   BEST FOR: Broad targeting, community engagement, and businesses seeking an older, more diverse audience.

2. **Instagram**: Want to tell your brand's story through stunning visuals? Instagram's got you covered. With 2 billion monthly active users, mostly aged 18-34, it's ideal for businesses in lifestyle, fashion, and beauty. Whether it's images, Stories, or reels, Instagram is the go-to for visual storytelling and influencer-driven content.
   BEST FOR: Visual storytelling, lifestyle brands, and businesses targeting younger audiences.

3. **TikTok**: If you want to connect with Gen Z and create content that goes viral, TikTok is where you need to be. With 1.6 billion monthly users, it's especially popular among 18-24-year-olds. The short-form video format is great for brands that want to be creative, fun, and make a quick impact.
   BEST FOR: Short-form video, viral marketing, and engaging Gen Z and younger millennials.

4. **LinkedIn**: If you're looking to connect with professionals and decision-makers, LinkedIn is where you want to be. With 310 million monthly users, it's perfect for B2B marketing and reaching industry leaders. LinkedIn also excels at lead generation, making it the top platform for B2B marketers.
    BEST FOR: B2B marketing, professional services, and networking.

5. **YouTube**: Got valuable expertise to share? YouTube is your platform. With 2.5 billion monthly active users, it's popular across all age groups, especially 18-34-year-olds. Whether it's educational content, tutorials, or entertainment, YouTube helps businesses engage audiences on a deeper level through long-form video.
    BEST FOR: Long-form video content, tutorials, and building brand awareness.

6. **X (formerly Twitter)**: Need to share real-time updates or be part of trending conversations? X is great for that. With 586 million users, it's all about fast interactions, making it ideal for businesses that thrive on quick customer service and trend-driven discussions.
    BEST FOR: Real-time engagement, customer service, and trend-driven content.

7. **Threads**: Looking to foster real-time conversations in a more intimate setting? Threads, Meta's new platform, is gaining traction with younger users, particularly those already active on Instagram. It's perfect for building deeper connections and engaging with your community.
    BEST FOR: Real-time discussions and businesses looking to foster deeper connections with their audience.

8. **Pinterest**: If your brand is all about visual discovery—think home decor, fashion, or food—Pinterest is your spot. With 518 million monthly users, predominantly women, it's the ideal place for showcasing products in a visually inspiring way and driving discovery.
    BEST FOR: Visual discovery, e-commerce, and brands targeting women in lifestyle and creative sectors.

CREATING CONSISTENTLY ENGAGING CONTENT

Social media is about more than just posting; it's about connecting with your audience and communicating your core messages consistently. The most important advice when it comes to content creation is this: it's not about what you want to say; it's about what your customer wants to hear.

When you produce content that is useful, interesting, or exciting to your customers, they are much more likely to engage. And while some of your audience may already be familiar with your brand and ready to buy, others may still be in the early stages of their customer journey. This is why it's crucial to create content that speaks to customers at every stage of the sales funnel.

To achieve this, organize your content into four key pillars:
- **Brand Awareness**
- **Consideration**
- **Sales**
- **Advocate**

Each pillar addresses a different aspect of your audience's journey, helping to nurture potential customers and retain existing ones.

Brand Awareness Content
Connecting with Your Audience

Brand awareness content focuses on introducing your brand to new audiences and reinforcing your presence with existing customers. This is your opportunity to create engaging, sociable content that isn't directly about selling but about creating brand impressions. The goal is to make your audience familiar with your brand's logo, colours, and personality.

TOP TIP: Keep your posts brief and visual—images and videos featuring real people tend to reach twice as many viewers as generic visuals.

Here are a few content ideas to get started (choose what's most authentic to your brand):

1. **Company Updates**: Let your audience know what's happening—new hires, milestones, behind-the-scenes changes. It helps build a sense of familiarity.

2. **Motivation and Quotes**: Share an inspiring quote and connect it to your brand's values or a personal story.

3. **Trending News in Your Industry**: Post about current events or trends in your niche to keep your audience informed.

4. **Thought Leadership Insights**: Share your perspective on industry trends, best practices, or challenges. Let people see you as an authority in your field.

5. **Stories from Your Past**: Share stories that have shaped your career or your company—people love hearing about your journey and what drives you.

6. **Out and About at Networking Events**: Post photos or videos from conferences, networking events, or industry gatherings to show your involvement in the community.

7. **Speaking Engagements**: If you're speaking at an event, share highlights to build credibility and encourage more engagement.

8. **Inspirational Stories**: Tell a story that resonates emotionally with your audience—something that inspires or uplifts them.

9. **Your Opinion on Relevant Topics**: Share your thoughts on hot topics in your industry. Being open about your perspective helps position your brand and invites others to engage.

10. **Behind the Scenes**: People love to see the view of your office/premises that they don't normally get to see.

Consideration Content

Building Authority and Trust

Consideration content positions your brand as an expert in your field. By offering advice, how-tos, or education, you help your audience see your brand as a valuable resource. This type of content is often called expert content and helps build trust with potential customers who may still be in the research phase.

Consider presenting this content through videos, reels, or multi-image swipe posts to boost engagement. Here are 10 ideas for consideration content:

1. **Top Tips**: Share practical tips related to your industry.
2. **FAQ Answers**: Answer frequently asked questions about your products or services in short videos or graphics.
3. **How-To Tutorials**: Demonstrate a process or product usage step-by-step.
4. **Ask Me Anything**: Engage with your audience by allowing them to ask questions in real-time.
5. **Common Mistakes**: Share common pitfalls customers might face and how to avoid them.
6. **Industry Insights**: Share key trends or forecasts in your niche.
7. **Life Hacks**: Provide time-saving tips or clever ideas related to your industry.
8. **Do's and Don'ts**: Offer advice on what to avoid and what to embrace in your niche.
9. **Interviews with Experts**: Feature influential figures in your industry to add credibility.
10. **New Trends**: Highlight the latest trends and how they impact your audience.

Sales Content
Sometimes We're Selling

Sales content is designed to convert leads into customers. It should focus on the benefits of your product or service and compel the reader to take action. Whether you're promoting an eBook, a digital course, or a physical product, ensure that your sales posts address the key pain points of your audience and how your solution solves them.

Every sales post should have one clear Call to Action (CTA)—something simple and direct, like "Call Now," "Sign Up Today," or "Buy Now." Avoid overwhelming your audience with too many options.

TOP TIP: Be concise, persuasive, and make it easy for your audience to understand what action they should take next.

Here are some sales content ideas:

1. **New Product/Service Announcements**: Use images or videos to introduce new offerings.

2. **Free Lead Magnet**: Share a downloadable resource, such as an eBook or guide, to capture leads.

3. **Sneak Peeks**: Tease upcoming launches with a short video or image carousel.

4. **Holiday Sales**: Capitalize on seasonal events with limited-time offers.

5. **Free Products/Services**: Promote giveaways or special deals to entice action.

6. **Flash Sales**: Create urgency with a 24-hour sale or special discount.

Advocate Content
Letting Your Customers Speak for You

Advocate content highlights testimonials and reviews from your happiest customers. People trust recommendations from other customers more than a brand's self-promotion, so leveraging this content can significantly boost your credibility.

Encourage customers to share their experiences through reviews, recommendations, or video testimonials. Make it easy for them by providing simple ways to leave feedback on platforms like Facebook, LinkedIn, Google, or your website. Additionally, handpick satisfied customers to share video reviews or feature their success stories in your content.

TOP TIP: Video testimonials are highly effective—compile a collection of short, authentic reviews from your advocates to showcase on your social media pages.

Here are some advocate content ideas:

1. **Customer Success Stories**: Feature images and quotes from customers who've had great results using your product.

2. **Customer Testimonials**: Share video testimonials or quotes from satisfied clients.

3. **Nominations or Awards**: Celebrate customer nominations, certifications, or awards to build social proof.

4. **Media Features**: Repost any media mentions or features that highlight your business.

5. **Influencer Posts**: Repost content created by influencers who endorse your products.

USING VIDEO FOR SOCIAL MEDIA SUCCESS

Video is taking over social media, and platforms like Instagram, TikTok, and YouTube are all about it—whether it's reels, short-form clips, or live streams. Videos can really boost your engagement and help you connect with your audience on a deeper level.

Here's how to make your video content shine and some best practices for optimising it across different platforms:

1. **Embrace Short-Form Vertical Videos (Reels and TikToks)**: Short-form vertical videos are quick, fun, and super engaging, especially on Instagram and TikTok. LinkedIn introduced a new vertical video feed in late 2024, offering the potential to stand out in this newsfeed if you have the right strategy and content. These bite-sized clips are great for showcasing your products, giving behind-the-scenes peeks, or highlighting user-generated content.

Best Practices:

- **Keep It Short and Snappy**: Aim for 15-30 seconds to quickly grab attention.
- **Hook Them Fast**: Start with something eye-catching to stop the scroll—an exciting fact, a bold statement, or a fun visual.
- **Use Trends**: Trending music, challenges, or filters can help your video reach a bigger audience.
- **Add Captions**: Many people watch videos without sound, so captions make your content accessible and engaging.

2. **Optimize for Each Platform**: Every social media platform has its own vibe, so tailoring your videos to fit each one is key to getting the most engagement.

- **Instagram**: Reels are all about short, vertical videos. Make them visually appealing and fast-paced to align with your brand's identity.
  TOP TIP: Use Instagram's in-app editing tools to add text, music, and trendy filters.

- **Facebook**: Facebook reels are ideal for reaching a broader audience. Create videos that are attention-grabbing but friendly and relatable.
  TOP TIP: Use captions to improve accessibility and engagement, and consider using Facebook's in-app tools to add effects.

- **TikTok**: TikTok loves creativity and authenticity. The more real and unpolished your content feels, the better.
  TOP TIP: Jump on viral trends and challenges, but make sure they fit your brand's message.

- **YouTube Shorts**: YouTube's version of short-form content is perfect for storytelling in a bit more depth.
  TOP TIP: Always add a strong call-to-action (CTA) at the end—encourage viewers to subscribe, watch more content, or visit your website.

- **LinkedIn Video**: LinkedIn's vertical video feed is a great opportunity for professional and educational content. Keep it informative and aligned with your industry.
  TOP TIP: Add captions for a polished touch, and consider including insights, tips, or a clear value statement to encourage shares and saves.

3. **Make the Most of Live Streaming**: Live streaming is an amazing way to connect with your audience in real-time. Whether it's a product launch, a Q&A, or a behind-the-scenes tour, live video feels more personal and builds a sense of community.

Best Practices:

- **Announce Ahead of Time**: Let people know when you'll be going live so they can plan to join.
- **Engage in Real-Time**: Chat with viewers, answer questions, and make it a conversation.
- **Provide Value**: Share exclusive content, offer live demos, or give updates that feel personal and relevant.

4. **Focus on Storytelling**: Storytelling is key to making your videos resonate. Whether it's a short clip or a live stream, focus on delivering a message that connects emotionally. Videos that tell a story, solve a problem, or show how your brand fits into your audience's lives are the ones that drive engagement.

   TOP TIP: Use customer testimonials, success stories, or even personal anecdotes to make a real connection with your audience.

5. **Analyse and Optimize**: Every platform gives you analytics to see what's working and what's not. Pay attention to metrics like views, likes, comments, and shares to adjust your video strategy accordingly.

   TOP TIP: If a particular style of video is working, do more of that! Always experiment, but let data guide your decisions.

THE POWER OF MULTI-SCENE SHORT-FORM VIDEOS: KEEP VIEWERS ENGAGED

A hot trend in short-form videos is using multiple scenes, with each scene delivering a single point. This style is great for keeping viewers engaged—especially when you switch up settings, angles, or use quick transitions. TikTok, Instagram reels, and YouTube Shorts all thrive on this kind of fast-paced, dynamic content.

LinkedIn introduced a new vertical video feed in late 2024, offering the potential to stand out in this newsfeed if you have the right strategy and content.

Why Multi-Scene Videos Work:

1. **Enhanced Engagement**: Quick scene changes keep the content fresh, preventing viewers from losing interest.
2. **Varied Settings**: Switching backgrounds or environments makes your video visually appealing and helps keep it interesting.
3. **Relatable and Authentic**: Filming while walking or talking from your car gives a casual vibe, making the content feel more spontaneous and genuine.
4. **Retaining Attention**: Every new scene keeps viewers curious about what's next, helping you keep them watching until the end.

Tips for Creating Multi-Scene Videos:

- **Record in Different Locations**: Switch it up—start in your living room, move to the kitchen, or take a walk outside. It keeps the video dynamic.
- **Use Movement**: Recording while walking adds immediacy and feels more personal. Filming from your car can make the content feel more real-time.

- **Short Sentences, Quick Transitions**: Keep each scene concise and use transitions like cuts or swipes to keep things visually interesting.
- **Multiple Camera Angles**: If you're in one location, change up the angles—try close-ups, wide shots, or slight shifts to keep the visuals engaging.

Examples of Multi-Scene Videos:

- **Vlogging**: Switching scenes while sharing updates keeps the story engaging.
- **Product Demonstrations**: Highlight different features in different scenes to keep the video dynamic.
- **Educational Content**: Break down complex topics into short, easy-to-understand bits across different scenes.

TIPS FOR RECORDING ENGAGING VIDEOS

Here are some best practices to make sure your videos stand out and keep viewers hooked:

1. **Optimize Your Lighting**: Natural light is your best friend for crisp, clear videos. Avoid harsh overhead lights, and position yourself near a window when filming indoors. Outdoors, a cloudy day can provide perfect, diffused lighting.

   TOP TIP: Avoid overhead lights that create shadows. If recording indoors, find a spot with soft natural light. For audio, stay away from echoey rooms—soft furnishings help absorb sound.

2. **Minimize Distractions**: Background noise can make or break your video. Be mindful of things like wind, traffic, or other noises that could distract your audience.

   TOP TIP: Light wind can sound loud on camera, so use an external mic if needed. If you add music, make sure it's copyright-free.

3. **Camera and Sound Settings**: Always check your camera settings before you start filming—make sure you're in HD for the best quality. Wipe your camera lens clean, and use a tripod or selfie stick to avoid shaky footage.

   TOP TIP: Avoid zooming in; it reduces video quality. Move closer instead. Keep the mic close and the camera steady for the best sound and visuals.

4. **Engage Your Audience**: The first three seconds are crucial to hook viewers. Start with something that grabs their attention—smile, look directly into the lens, and lead with a benefit or compelling story.

   TOP TIP: Smile and make eye contact with the camera to create a sense of connection. If you're batch-recording videos, change your outfit between takes to make each one feel fresh.

5.   **Plan Your Content**: Good videos tell a story or highlight a benefit. When planning, focus on the emotional benefits before diving into features.
     EXAMPLE: If promoting a product, start with how it makes people feel (the joy of receiving a gift) before talking about the details.

Quick Checklist for Filming High-Quality Videos:

- Use natural lighting; avoid overly bright or dark settings.
- Watch out for background noise and distractions.
- Film in HD; clean your lens and use a tripod.
- Avoid using zoom—move closer instead.
- Look into the lens, smile, and grab attention in the first few seconds.
- Plan your content around emotional benefits before introducing features.

HOW TO MAKE YOUR SOCIAL MEDIA POSTS STAND OUT

How you present your posts on social media can have a huge impact on how far they reach. Social media platforms use algorithms to decide what content gets seen, and these algorithms love posts that get engagement right after they're published. Think of likes, comments, views, and clicks as little votes that tell the algorithm your content is worth showing to more people.

Crafting Effective Social Media Post Descriptions
The way you create your social media posts can make all the difference in how many people see them. When platforms see that your post quickly gets likes, comments, and other interactions, they tend to show it to more users.

Here's a handy checklist to help you get the most out of each post:

1. **Timing Matters**: Pick the right day and time to publish your post. Make sure your audience is online and ready to engage— whether that's liking, commenting, sharing, clicking, or viewing your post.
2. **Visual Appeal**: Use eye-catching visuals to grab attention as people scroll. Posts featuring real people from your company tend to do especially well.
3. **Variety is Key**: Mix up your content types—short videos, single images, carousel posts—keeping your feed fresh and engaging.
4. **Direct Links**: Include direct links to products or guide visitors on how to make a purchase. Make it as easy as possible for your audience to buy from you.
5. **Use Links Sparingly**: Only include links when absolutely necessary. Sometimes posting a link in the comments can improve the post's performance.
6. **Mix Content Types**: Create a mix of content—brand awareness, consideration, sales, and advocate content—to address all stages of your audience's journey.

7. **Engaging Descriptions**: Craft your post descriptions carefully. The first line should grab attention and make people want to keep reading. Add extra insights to enhance the message.

8. **Clear CTA**: Include one clear call to action so your audience knows what to do next.

9. **Harness Hashtags**: Use relevant hashtags to expand your reach and help new people discover your content.

10. **Strategic Tagging**: Tag other relevant accounts, locations, or products to capture attention and potentially encourage sharing.

15 Call-To-Action Prompts to Boost Engagement

1. Save this post for later
2. Share if you found this post useful
3. Drop an emoji if you agree
4. Click the link in bio...
5. Follow for more updates
6. Comment below and let me know your thoughts on...
7. Double tap if you agree
8. Hit the ❤️ if you agree
9. Share this with someone who will benefit
10. Tag a friend
11. Swipe to learn more
12. Take a screenshot
13. DM me
14. Watch till the end
15. Repost to your story if...

SOCIAL MEDIA ALGORITHM INSIGHTS: ENGAGEMENT OVER FOLLOWERS

In 2025, social media algorithms are focusing more on what people are interested in rather than who they follow. This means that the visibility of your content depends more on engagement metrics—like likes, comments, shares, and meaningful interactions—than just your follower count. Whether it's LinkedIn, Instagram, TikTok, or Facebook, the algorithms are all about showing users content that matches their interests and behaviour. Let's dive deeper into this trend and see how it affects your content strategy.

1. **LinkedIn Algorithm: Prioritizing Engagement and Relevance**: LinkedIn's algorithm has evolved to prioritize content based on relevance, expertise, and engagement. It surfaces content that fits users' professional interests, giving more weight to meaningful comments from people in their network or industry. LinkedIn wants posts that add value—sharing insights, knowledge, and professional advice.

   KEY STAT: Posts that get early engagement (within the first hour of posting) are much more likely to be boosted in other users' feeds, giving them greater visibility. Plus, LinkedIn posts with images tend to get more comments, and those with native videos see five times the engagement of text-only posts (Sprout Social).

2. **Engagement Drives Visibility on All Platforms**: Across social media, content that sparks high engagement—comments, shares, reactions—gets pushed to more people. For example, Instagram's Explore page and TikTok's For You page are designed to show users content they interact with, not just content from accounts they follow.

   KEY STAT: On TikTok, 73% of users discover new brands through the For You page, based on content they engage with—even if they don't follow those accounts (Sprout Social). Facebook and Instagram also reward engagement, with posts that foster meaningful interactions seeing up to 60% more reach (Buffer).

3. **Best Practices for Maximizing Engagement**: To make the most of these algorithms, you need to create content that encourages interactions. Here are some tips for boosting engagement:

    • **LinkedIn** Share valuable content that's relevant to your industry. Ask questions to spark discussions and tag people in your network who can add to the conversation. Use native video or high-quality visuals to increase engagement. LinkedIn values meaningful comments and thoughtful discussions over simple likes or "congrats" comments.

    • **Instagram and TikTok** Create eye-catching content that grabs attention in the first three seconds. Jump on trends, challenges, or add interactive elements like polls to drive engagement. Strong calls to action—like "Comment below!" or "Tag a friend!"—can prompt more user interaction.

    • **All Platforms** Timing matters. Post when your audience is most active to get that crucial early engagement.

4. **Interest-Based vs. Follower-Based Content**: With the shift from follower-based to interest-based content, users can see your posts even if they don't follow you—as long as the algorithm finds it relevant. That means creating engaging, interaction-driven content is more important than ever for reaching beyond your immediate follower base.

THE IMPORTANCE OF SOCIAL MEDIA ENGAGEMENT

Social media engagement isn't just about posting content—it's about building real relationships with your audience and sparking meaningful interactions that boost your visibility and influence across platforms. From likes and comments to shares, saves, and direct messages, engagement is how both you and your followers connect, and it's a key indicator of how well your content resonates.

1. **Why Social Media Engagement Matters**: The more people interact with your brand, the more they start to recognize and remember you. Social media platforms use engagement as a major factor to decide which content gets pushed out to a wider audience. Posts that get lots of engagement—likes, comments, shares—are rewarded with more reach, meaning your content gets seen by even more people.

2. **What is Social Media Engagement?**: Social media engagement is all about how users interact with your content. This includes likes, comments, shares, saves, mentions, direct messages, and reposts. It also involves how you engage with others' content, which helps expand your visibility beyond just your followers.

   • **When Others Engage with Your Content**: High engagement means your content is hitting the mark with your audience. This boosts your reach, helps establish credibility, and makes a great impression on potential clients or collaborators.

   • **When You Engage with Others' Content**: Leaving thoughtful comments on others' posts can get you noticed by both the original poster and their audience. Engaging meaningfully with content in your industry helps you build relationships, grow your network, and position yourself as a thought leader.

3. **Elevate Your Profile by Engaging with Others**: If you want to achieve your goals on social media—whether that's attracting new customers, getting media coverage, or positioning yourself as an expert—engagement is key. One of the best ways to elevate your

profile is by interacting with others' content. This could mean liking and commenting on posts from potential customers, suppliers, or industry leaders, or joining in conversations under relevant hashtags.

TOP TIP: Make a list of key accounts you want to engage with regularly, and turn on notifications for their posts so you don't miss a chance to interact. Consistent engagement will help keep you top of mind for these connections.

4. **Create an Engagement Strategy**: To sustain and grow your social media presence, you need a solid engagement strategy. Here are some best practices to keep in mind:

   - **Engage Thoughtfully**: Leave meaningful comments that show genuine interest and spark conversation. Avoid generic or AI-generated responses—they're easy to spot and can feel insincere.

   - **Share and Mention**: Share relevant content from others and mention the original creators. This broadens your network and builds community.

   - **Be Consistent**: Regular engagement is crucial. Set aside time each day to connect with your audience and interact with other accounts in your industry. This consistency helps build relationships and improves your visibility.

5. **Measure Your Success**: Tracking your engagement metrics is vital to understanding how well your strategy is working. Keep an eye on profile views, new followers, comments, and direct messages to see if your engagement efforts are leading to meaningful connections. On platforms like LinkedIn, you can even see who's viewed your profile, giving you insights into how effective your engagement is.

   TOP TIP: Regularly check your profile views and engagement rates, and adjust your strategy as needed. If these metrics are consistently improving, it's a good sign that your engagement strategy is working.

THE POWER OF PAID ADVERTISING ON SOCIAL MEDIA

Paid advertising on social media is a powerful way to reach a much larger audience than organic posts alone. With organic reach becoming less predictable due to algorithm changes and increased competition, relying solely on unpaid content often isn't enough to generate significant sales or leads. By adding paid ads to your social media strategy, you can expand your reach and have more control over who sees your content, making it easier to connect with the right people at the right time.

Why Paid Ads Matter

Organic reach on social media has been steadily declining—platforms like Facebook now show your unpaid posts to only a small fraction of your audience. That's why paid ads are so important for boosting your visibility and getting real results.

Here's a telling example: to generate 10 sales from your website, you might need to reach about 25,000 people. This is based on an average click-through rate (CTR) of 2% and a typical conversion rate for website visitors. While increasing your CTR and conversion rate is always the goal, this shows that reaching a small audience with a single post usually isn't enough to drive significant sales.

Meta's Ad Targeting Capabilities

Meta's algorithm has come a long way, making ad targeting even more effective. Meta now uses automated ad targeting to retarget people who have already interacted with your content—whether they've engaged with your organic posts or previous ads. This means your ad spend is used more efficiently, reaching people who are most likely to convert based on their past behaviour.

Maximizing Your Budget

Whether it's building brand awareness, driving website traffic, or generating leads, the value you get from your budget depends on how well you target your audience, how engaging your content is, and how clear your messaging is.

When you run ads, your budget is influenced by how people engage with them. The more interactions your ad gets—likes, comments, shares, clicks—the further it will be shown to other potential customers. That's why high-quality, relevant ads tend to give you better performance and a higher return on investment (ROI).

Types of Paid Ads to Consider

Each platform offers different types of ads, and your choice will depend on your goals:

- **Facebook & Instagram Ads**: Great for targeting specific demographics or interests. You can use photo, video, carousel, or story ads to reach a bigger audience.
- **LinkedIn Ads**: Perfect for B2B marketers. LinkedIn ads let you target professionals by industry, job title, or company size.
- **TikTok Ads**: Ideal for reaching a younger audience. TikTok ads use short-form video to engage viewers.
- **YouTube Ads**: Video ads on YouTube can appear before videos or as recommended content, helping you reach an audience that's already watching video content.

How to Get the Most Out of Paid Ads

To make sure your ad budget is well spent, here are a few tips for success:

1. **Use advanced targeting features to reach the right people**: Filter by demographics, interests, and behaviours to connect with those most likely to engage with your brand.

2. **Test Your Ads**: Run A/B tests with different visuals, copy, and calls to action (CTAs) to see what resonates best with your audience.

3. **Creative and Messaging Matter**: Make sure your ads are visually appealing and your message is clear. Ads that speak to your audience's needs and emotions tend to perform better.

4 **Boost Your Best Performers**: If you notice an organic post doing really well, consider putting some ad spend behind it to reach an even bigger audience.

Continuous Monitoring and Adjustment

A successful paid ad strategy is all about continuous optimization. Review your campaigns regularly to track performance metrics like CTR, engagement, and conversions. If a campaign isn't delivering the results you want, tweak your targeting, adjust the visuals, or refine your message to improve performance.

By keeping a close eye on your campaigns and making adjustments along the way, you can ensure you're getting the most out of your budget and reaching your business goals.

REVIEWING YOUR SOCIAL MEDIA PERFORMANCE

Taking the time to regularly review how your social media content is performing—both organic and paid—is so important for understanding what really clicks with your audience. By using data to make decisions, you can refine your strategy, make better use of your resources, and improve your campaigns' effectiveness. Every social media platform provides valuable stats and insights into how your posts and campaigns are doing. Usually, you'll see an Insights or Analytics button under each post that gives you key performance metrics.

In addition to individual post performance, each platform has an Insights or Analytics section where you can get a broader overview of how your content and campaigns are doing. Some platforms offer more detailed insights than others, but it's worth getting familiar with what each platform offers so you can make the best decisions for your future campaigns.

Key Metrics to Track

1. **Reach**: This metric shows how many unique users have seen your post or ad. If your reach is low, it might be time to adjust your targeting or content strategy to expand your audience.

2. **Impressions**: Impressions tell you how many times your content has been displayed, even if it's to the same person multiple times. This helps you gauge your overall content exposure.

3. **Engagement**: Engagement includes actions like likes, comments, shares, and reactions. The more engagement your content receives, the more likely it is to be shown to a larger audience.

4. **Clicks**: Clicks indicate how many users clicked on your post, ad, or link. It's a good sign of deeper interest and engagement.

5. **Click-Through Rate (CTR)**: CTR measures how effective your post is at getting users to take action. It's calculated by dividing the number of clicks by the number of impressions.

6. **Conversion Rate**: Some platforms, especially those integrated with eCommerce like Facebook and Instagram, track conversions—whether it's a product purchase or a form fill—helping you understand how your content is impacting your business goals.

7. **Return on Investment (ROI)**: Platforms like Facebook's Ads Manager help you track ROI by comparing the revenue generated by your ads to the amount spent, helping you see if your campaigns are profitable.

8. **Customer Acquisition Cost (CAC)**: CAC is calculated by dividing your total marketing spend by the number of new customers acquired. This helps you track how much it costs to bring in new customers through your paid ads.

9. **Customer Lifetime Value (CLV)**: While not directly available on most social platforms, you can calculate CLV by combining social media insights with customer data from your CRM. This helps you understand the long-term value of your campaigns.

10. **Social Media Traffic**: Google Analytics and other tracking tools can help you see how much traffic your website gets from social media. Some platforms, like Facebook and Instagram, also provide insights into which posts are driving the most traffic.

Platform-Specific Insights and How to Use Them

*   **Facebook & Instagram**: Both platforms provide in-depth insights through Meta Business Suite. You can track metrics like reach, impressions, engagement, and conversions, along with audience demographics. This information can help you better target your future campaigns.

*   **LinkedIn**: LinkedIn's analytics focus on engagement and demographics. You can see which industries, job titles, and companies are interacting with your content, which is especially useful for B2B marketing.

- **Twitter (X)**: Twitter's Analytics Dashboard offers a snapshot of tweet impressions, engagements, and engagement rate. While not as detailed as other platforms, it still gives you a good idea of how your content is performing.

- **YouTube**: YouTube provides metrics like watch time, engagement, and subscriber growth. These insights can help you understand how successful your video content is and adjust your strategy accordingly.

- **TikTok**: TikTok's Pro Account analytics give you data on video views, profile views, and follower demographics. Engagement metrics like likes, comments, and shares are key to growing your presence on the platform.

Turning Metrics into Actionable Insights

The metrics you track are more than just numbers—they're valuable insights that can help shape your future campaigns. Here's how to use them effectively:

- **Identify Patterns**: Pay attention to when your audience is most active and which content formats (videos, images, stories) perform best. Platforms like Facebook and Instagram provide insights on the best times to post, which can help you optimize your schedule.

- **Understand Audience Preferences**: Look at engagement data to see which posts or ads resonate most with your audience. This lets you tailor your messaging and visuals to maximize impact.

- **Refine Content and Messaging**: If certain types of content aren't performing well, review your insights to figure out why. Adjust your visuals, headlines, or calls to action to improve future results.

Short-Term vs. Long-Term Metrics

While short-term metrics like engagement and CTR give you immediate feedback, long-term metrics like Customer Lifetime Value (CLV) and brand loyalty are just as important. These show the lasting impact of your social media campaigns and help you measure long-term growth and retention.

Data-Driven Decision Making

Reviewing your social media metrics regularly ensures your strategy is based on data, not just guesswork. Each platform offers insights to help you see what's working and what needs improvement. By consistently tracking these metrics and making informed adjustments, you can optimize your social media efforts, making sure your campaigns are efficient, impactful, and aligned with your business goals.

Remember, the insights each platform provides aren't just numbers—they're the keys to unlocking your social media success. By analysing, testing, and refining your strategy based on these insights, you can keep improving your campaigns and drive even greater results.

THE GROWTH OF AI IN SOCIAL MEDIA MARKETING

AI can be your secret weapon for getting content done faster—without losing that personal touch. In recent years, AI has made a significant impact on social media marketing, transforming how businesses create, schedule, and optimize their content. These tools have become game-changers, with the AI market projected to reach $126 billion by 2025.

Marketers are embracing AI at an increasing rate—80% are now using some form of AI technology to optimize campaigns and improve targeting. AI tools like ChatGPT, Canva's Magic Studio, and Descript help marketers generate content quickly, automate repetitive tasks, and analyse audience engagement more efficiently. From automatically generated captions to AI-enhanced visuals, these tools allow for higher productivity and better data-driven decisions.

That said, while AI offers amazing opportunities to enhance your marketing strategy, it's important to keep your unique voice, creativity, and personal style at the centre of it all. AI can help streamline content creation and editing, but your ideas and personality are what truly make your content stand out.

Relying too heavily on AI could make your content feel formulaic or generic.". Remember, your audience values authentic connections, and it's your unique perspective that sets you apart. Use AI to assist in your process, but always add your personal touch, ideas, and brand personality to keep your content authentic and engaging.

In the ever-evolving world of social media marketing, AI is a powerful ally—but it's your originality that will continue to drive lasting engagement and success.

TOP AI TOOLS FOR SOCIAL MEDIA MARKETING IN 2025

AI can be your secret weapon for getting content done faster—without losing that personal touch. These tools have become essential for social media marketing, making it easier than ever to create, edit, and manage your content. Below is an updated list of the top AI tools for content creation, video editing, and image generation, including Opus.pro and CapCut.

1. AI Tools for Content Creation

- **ChatGPT**: A versatile tool for content generation, ChatGPT helps marketers write engaging social media posts, blog content, and even email copy. It's great for brainstorming and automating responses to user comments.
  Use Case: Generate creative Instagram captions or LinkedIn posts tailored to specific tones or industries.

- **Jasper**: Jasper excels at writing both short-form social media content and long-form blog posts, with highly customizable outputs based on your prompts.
  Use Case: Create SEO-optimized blog posts or high-conversion Facebook ads with minimal effort.

- **Copy.ai**: This tool specializes in creating copy for ads, emails, and social media, helping you generate engaging content quickly with AI-based templates.
  Use Case: Generate ad copy for Facebook or Instagram campaigns focused on driving conversions.

2   AI Tools for Video Editing

- **Descript**: A favourite for podcasters and video creators, Descript uses AI to make video and audio editing simple. Edit videos by modifying text transcripts and add features like automatic captioning.
  Use Case: Edit podcast episodes and create social media teasers by easily removing filler words and cutting down clips.

- **Pictory**: Pictory turns long-form content into short, shareable video clips. It's perfect for repurposing blog posts, webinars, or long videos into content suited for Instagram or LinkedIn.
  Use Case: Repurpose a 30-minute webinar into multiple short clips optimized for social media sharing.

- **Opus.pro**: Opus.pro automatically generates short-form clips from long videos, making it perfect for creating social media highlights. It selects key moments and adds captions to make video editing much faster.
  Use Case: Turn a full-length podcast into multiple TikTok or Instagram clips with automated editing and captions.

- **CapCut**: Developed by ByteDance, CapCut is loved by TikTok creators but is also widely used for general video editing across platforms. With AI features like automatic captions, background removal, and motion tracking, it makes editing simple and effective.
  Use Case: Edit TikTok or Instagram videos with advanced features like motion tracking and background effects—no professional skills required.

3   AI Tools for Image Creation

- **Canva** (Magic Studio): Canva's Magic Studio tool uses AI to generate templates and suggest colour schemes, fonts, and layouts based on your brand. It's perfect for creating social media graphics quickly.
  Use Case: Small businesses can create Instagram posts and Stories that maintain consistent brand visuals without hiring a designer.

- **DALL·E**: DALL·E generates custom images from text descriptions, allowing you to create unique visuals that stand out from typical stock photos. It's great for adding a creative twist to your visual content.
  Use Case: Generate one-of-a-kind images for social media posts or ad campaigns that stand out from the crowd.

- **Adobe Firefly**: Integrated into Adobe's design ecosystem, Firefly allows you to create high-quality images and graphics with minimal input, making it a powerful tool for streamlining your workflow.
  Use Case: Create custom visual content for ad campaigns using Adobe Firefly's AI-driven image generation capabilities.

These AI tools can make your content creation process faster, more efficient, and more creative—but remember to always add your personal touch to keep your content authentic and uniquely yours.

SUPERCHARGE YOUR CONTENT STRATEGY WITH CHATGPT PROMPTS

Boost Productivity with ChatGPT and Custom GPTs

ChatGPT is an incredibly powerful tool for content creation, enabling you to increase productivity while generating high-quality content tailored to your business. Below, you'll find prompts and techniques designed to maximize ChatGPT's potential—whether you're building buyer personas, crafting social posts, or creating emails. By creating custom GPTs for specific needs, you can enhance this tool's ability to deliver more targeted and effective results for your brand. Ready to dive in? Let's explore how to use ChatGPT and custom GPTs to level up your social media strategy!

Prompts to Build B2B and B2C Buyer Personas

Creating detailed buyer personas is key to understanding your audience. These persona prompts help ChatGPT generate in-depth profiles based on your specific B2B or B2C needs.

B2B Buyer Persona Prompt

Use this prompt to build a detailed persona of a potential B2B client. Tailoring ChatGPT to craft personas based on job roles and industry will help you connect with your audience on a deeper level.

Prompt: Create a detailed persona for a [job title] working in [industry, company size, location]. This persona faces the following challenges: [list researched challenges]. They are considering [product or service] and need help with [specific pain points]. List their goals, aspirations, concerns, emotional triggers, and decision criteria for choosing a company like mine.

B2C Buyer Persona Prompt

This prompt helps you capture the emotional journey and core needs of your consumer audience.

Prompt: Create a persona for a [consumer type] who is seeking help with [pain points or desires]. They are considering [product or service] and need assistance with [list specific solutions]. Detail their goals, fears, emotional triggers, and the factors they will use to choose a product or service like mine.

Create Custom GPTs for Buyer Personas

To take personalization further, consider building a custom GPT specifically for your buyer personas. With a custom GPT, you can provide ChatGPT with specific persona details that will shape every piece of content it generates, creating consistency across social posts, emails, and ads.

1. **Why Create a Custom GPT for Buyer Personas?**: A custom GPT can store details about your ideal customers, ensuring that your content consistently aligns with the unique needs, pain points, and preferences of each audience segment. By creating a GPT based on detailed buyer personas, you'll have an intelligent assistant ready to generate messaging that resonates deeply with your target audience.

2. **How to Get Started**: Use ChatGPT's customization options to build a version tailored to your audience. Include:

   - **Persona Attributes**: Role, industry, goals, challenges, and decision-making factors.
   - **Tone and Style**: Preferred language, tone, and engagement style for each persona.
   - **Primary Motivators**: Emotional triggers, pain points, and buying criteria.

Example Prompt to Set Up Your Custom GPT*:* Create a custom GPT based on the following buyer persona: [Add persona details like job role, industry, goals, pain points, etc.]. This GPT should generate [social posts, emails, content ideas] in a [friendly/professional] tone, with messaging centered around [key interests or needs].

Training ChatGPT About Your Business

To receive relevant and personalized content, it's essential to "train" ChatGPT with details about your business. Here's a prompt to help ChatGPT understand your unique value:

Prompt*:* I am a [details about you and your business, including services and target audience]. My unique selling points include [list accolades or differentiators]. The tone I prefer is [e.g., conversational, professional, etc.]. My main business goal is to [goals such as growth, brand awareness, or customer acquisition].

Structuring Effective Prompts for ChatGPT

Strong prompts make all the difference in the quality of responses from ChatGPT or your custom GPT. Include details about who you are, your audience, and the content type you need. Here's a five-step structure to guide you:

Five-Step ChatGPT Prompt for Content Creation

1. I am [describe yourself and your business].
2. I am targeting [persona details].
3. Create a [social post, blog post, email, etc.].
4. Focus on [main topic and specific areas].
5. The tone should be [e.g., friendly, professional, etc.].

Persona-Driven Content and Critique with Custom GPTs

When developing content for specific buyer personas, your custom GPT can help tailor messaging to resonate with your target audience. Assign your persona a unique name—like "Eco-Minded Ella" or "Strategy Sam"—for easy reference. Save persona descriptions on your phone or computer for easy access, as ChatGPT doesn't retain memory across sessions.

To reference a saved persona, use a prompt like: "This is the persona Eco-Minded Ella," then copy and paste the persona details into your prompt. Ask for content ideas, critiques, or new drafts that align with that persona's needs.

Prompt examples:

- What will Eco-Minded Ella think of the attached lead magnet?
- How will Productive Jamie respond to this landing page?
- Please critique this email content in relation to Strategy Sam.

If you're using a paid version of ChatGPT that supports attachments, you can upload documents or link webpages for a more thorough review.

Crafting a Compelling Social Post

Looking to transform a story into an engaging social media post? Use this structure to create powerful posts for LinkedIn, Facebook, or Instagram:

Compelling Post Prompt: Rewrite the following text for a [LinkedIn, Facebook, Instagram] post, using this structure:

- **Hook**: Start with a bold question or engaging statement.
- **Story**: Share your experience, highlighting key events and emotions.
- **Lesson**: Share the main takeaway, tying it to your audience's needs or interests.
- **CTA**: End with a clear call to action that invites engagement.

ChatGPT for Summarizing Meetings and Improving Grammar
ChatGPT is also a helpful tool for summarizing key meeting points or refining your text. Here are some ways to use it effectively:

- Use the video transcript to summarize key points of this meeting.
- What advice did I give to [name] during the meeting?
- Using the main points of this meeting, write a blog post.
- Using the key points, write a nurturing email to my list.
- Check syntax and grammar of the following text.

Bonus Tip: Chat Like It's a Colleague!
Think of ChatGPT as a helpful colleague—give it clear instructions, request specific feedback, and don't hesitate to ask follow-up questions. This approach will make your interactions with ChatGPT (or your custom GPT) even more productive.

Don't miss my live training on **ChatGPT-Powered Content Strategy: Planning 2025's Social Media Success** taking place on Wednesday, January 22nd, at 11 am ET / 4 pm GMT. (playback available) (Value $218).

Claim $377 of free online resources at www.SellOnSocialMedia.Academy/2025Resources

AUTHENTICITY IN AN AI-DRIVEN WORLD

AI tools are transforming social media marketing, making everything faster and more precise. But as these tools become more common, staying true to who you are is more important than ever. Authenticity is what builds trust and long-lasting relationships with your audience. AI can help, but it should be there to support your ideas, not replace them.

Here are some top ways to keep things real in an AI-driven world:

1. **Use AI to Enhance Your Ideas, Not Replace Them**: AI is amazing for editing, improving, or polishing your ideas, but it shouldn't replace your voice. Your audience wants to hear from you, not from a machine. Use AI to help with things like refining your wording, finding the best posting times, or summarizing long texts—but always make sure your core message comes from you.

   TOP TIP: Write your posts yourself, then use AI tools like Grammarly or ChatGPT to fine-tune them. Let AI handle the grammar, but keep the ideas yours.

2. **Share Your Own Opinions**: One thing AI lacks is real opinions, emotions, and experiences—those things that make you relatable. Sharing your personal insights, challenges, and wins is a powerful way to connect with your audience. If you let AI do too much of the talking, your content might lose that personal touch people crave.

   TOP TIP: Share your unique perspective on industry trends, personal stories, and experiences. It's a great way to show authenticity in your posts.

3   **Use Real-Life Images and Videos**: In a world of AI-enhanced and airbrushed visuals, real images stand out. Instead of relying on AI-generated or overly polished content, show the real side of your business by sharing behind-the-scenes photos of you, your team, and your day-to-day. Genuine visuals help your audience connect with you on a personal level.

TOP TIP: Share behind-the-scenes moments, team celebrations, or casual shots of your workspace. For videos, you can use AI tools like CapCut to edit, but make sure the content reflects your brand's true personality.

4   **Let Your Personality Shine**: Your personality is one of your biggest strengths in building authentic connections. Don't hide behind stiff, overly formal language or AI-generated copy. Let your humour, quirks, and unique style come through in your posts. Whether you're sharing a thought on LinkedIn or posting an Instagram Story, let your personality be front and centre.

TOP TIP: Add personal stories, jokes, or casual language that reflects who you are. It'll make your posts more relatable and help you build a loyal following.

5   **Never Let AI Tools Comment for You**: One of the worst things you can do is let AI respond to comments or engage with your followers for you. People can spot automated replies from a mile away, and it just feels impersonal. Authentic engagement is about real conversations—whether you're answering a question, thanking someone, or replying to a comment. Hand-written replies build deeper connections.

TOP TIP: Set aside time to personally reply to comments and messages. It might take longer, but it strengthens your bond with your audience in a way that AI never could.

MAKING THE MOST OF YOUR SOCIAL MEDIA CONTENT CALENDAR

Using this social media content calendar can really take your social media marketing to the next level. Planning your content in advance brings a lot of great benefits:

1. **Reduced Stress and Enhanced Creativity**: Planning ahead means you're not scrambling at the last minute, which takes away a lot of the pressure. This extra breathing room allows for more creative thinking, leading to posts that are more engaging and innovative.

2. **Time Savings**: By dedicating specific blocks of time to plan and create your social media content, you'll actually save time in the long run. This helps you stay consistent and produce high-quality content more easily.

3. **Inspiration from Prompts**: The prompts provided in this calendar are a great source of inspiration. You can customize each prompt to align with your business's goals and values, keeping your posts relevant and purposeful.

4. **Diverse Content Opportunities**: The prompts cover a wide range of topics. Some will add a fun, light-hearted vibe to your brand, while others help you position yourself as an authority in your industry.

5. **Leverage Hashtags**: Don't forget to add relevant hashtags to your posts. This helps increase the visibility of your content, putting it in front of users who follow those hashtags and expanding your reach beyond your current followers.

6. **Global Reach**: These prompts are inspired by ideas from all over the world, giving you a chance to connect with a global audience. This is especially helpful if your business operates internationally or wants to grow beyond local borders.

To make the most of your content calendar, try to establish a regular routine for planning and creating content. Adapt the prompts to fit your brand's voice and messaging making sure every post serves a purpose in your overall marketing strategy. By using this calendar, you can boost your social media presence, connect with your audience in meaningful ways, and reach your marketing goals.

Alongside this powerful content calendar, there are other free resources available that can help you supercharge your online presence:

2025 Social Media Content Planning Calendar (Value $159) Download this calendar to keep your social media campaigns organized and on track. It's a great way to stay ahead of the game.

Claim $377 of free online resources at www.SellOnSocialMedia.Academy/2025Resources

2025
QUARTERLY & YEARLY
GOAL PLANS

ANNUAL GOALS AND PLANNING NOTES

January	February	March

April	May	June

July	August	September

October	November	December

QUARTER 1 GOALS AND PLANNING NOTES

January

February

March

QUARTER 2 GOALS AND PLANNING NOTES

April

May

June

QUARTER 3 GOALS AND PLANNING NOTES

July

August

September

QUARTER 4 GOALS AND PLANNING NOTES

October

November

December

2025
CONTENT
CALENDAR

 Sell OnSocial.Media

JANUARY 2025

Date	Day
Wed 01	New Year's Day
Thur 02	National Buffet Day World Introvert Day
Fri 03	Festival of Sleep Day
Sat 04	National Trivia Day World Braille Day
Sun 05	National Whipped Cream Day National Bird Day
Mon 06	Nollaig Na mBan National Cuddle Up Day National Technology Day
Tue 07	National Bobblehead Day National Tempura Day
Wed 08	National Bubble Bath Day National English Toffee Day National Winter Skin Relief Day World Typing Day
Thur 09	National Apricot Day National Law Enforcement Appreciation Day National Word Nerd Day
Fri 10	National Save The Eagles Day National Houseplant Appreciation Day
Sat 11	National Milk Day National Human Trafficking Awareness Day
Sun 12	National Pharmacist Day
Mon 13	National Gluten-Free Day National Sticker Day
Tue 14	National Dress Up Your Pet Day Organize Your Home Day

Date	Day
Wed 15	National Bagel Day National Strawberry Ice Cream Day
Thur 16	International Hot and Spicy Food Day
Fri 17	Kid Inventors' Day
Sat 18	National Thesaurus Day
Sun 19	World Religion Day National Popcorn Day
Mon 20	National Penguin Day National Cheese Lover's Day
Tue 21	National Hugging Day International Sweatpants Day
Wed 22	Celebration of Life Day
Thur 23	National Handwriting Day
Fri 24	National Compliment Day
Sat 25	National Irish Coffee Day
Sun 26	National Spouses Day National Green Juice Day
Mon 27	National Chocolate Cake Day
Tue 28	Data Privacy Day International Lego Day Global Community Engagement Day
Wed 29	National Puzzle Day National Corn Chip Day
Thur 30	National Croissant Day
Fri 31	National Inspire Your Heart With Art Day

Sun	Mon	Tue	Wed	Thu	Fri	Sat
			01	02	03	04
05	06	07	08	09	10	11
12	13	14	15	16	17	18
19	20	21	22	23	24	25
26	27	28	29	30	31	

> Notes

 Sell OnSocial.Media

Claim $377 of free online resources at www.SellOnSocialMedia.Academy/2025Resources

FEBRUARY 2025

Date	Day	Date	Day
Sat 01	Car Insurance Day Change Your Password Day National Get Up Day	Fri 14	St. Valentine's Day
Sun 02	Groundhog Day National Ukulele Day National Brown Dog Day	Sat 15	Digital Learning Day Singles Appreciation Day International Childhood Cancer Day
Mon 03	Doggy Date Night National Golden Retriever Day Feed the Birds Day	Sun 16	National Almond Day
		Mon 17	Random Acts of Kindness Day
Tue 04	World Cancer Day	Tue 18	National Drink Wine Day
Wed 05	World Read Out Loud Day	Wed 19	Tug of War Day National Chocolate Mint Day
Thur 06	National Optimists Day	Thur 20	World Day of Social Justice Love Your Pets Day
Fri 07	National Ballet Day		
Sat 08	Opera Day National Kite Flying Day	Fri 21	International Mother Language Day
Sun 09	National Pizza Day	Sat 22	National Walking the Dog Day World Thinking Day
Mon 10	National Umbrella Day Teddy Day International Epilepsy Day	Sun 23	National Banana Bread Day
		Mon 24	National Tortilla Chip Day
Tue 11	National Latte Day National Make a Friend Day International Day of Women and Girls in Science	Tue 25	World Spay Day
		Wed 26	Letter to an Elder Day National Tell a Fairy Tale Day National Pistachio Day
Wed 12	International Darwin Day	Thur 27	International Polar Bear Day National Strawberry Day
Thur 13	World Radio Day Galentine's Day	Fri 28	Rare Disease Day

Sun	Mon	Tue	Wed	Thu	Fri	Sat
						01
02	03	04	05	06	07	08
09	10	11	12	13	14	15
16	17	18	19	20	21	22
23	24	25	26	27	28	

> Notes

MARCH 2025

Date	Day
Sat 01	Self-Injury Awareness Day Zero Discrimination Day World Music Therapy Day
Sun 02	World Compliment Day World Teen Mental Wellness Day
Mon 03	World Hearing Day
Tue 04	National Sons Day World Obesity Day
Wed 05	Ash Wednesday
Thur 06	World Book Day National Dentist's Day National Oreo Cookie Day National Dress Day
Fri 07	Employee Appreciation Day National Be Heard Day
Sat 08	International Women's Day
Sun 09	National Meatball Day
Mon 10	National Pack Your Lunch Day
Tue 11	National Funeral Director and Mortician Recognition Day
Wed 12	National Girl Scout Day National Working Moms Day
Thur 13	National Good Samaritan Day World Kidney Day
Fri 14	World Sleep Day International Day of Mathematics
Sat 15	World Consumer Rights Day

Date	Day
Sun 16	National Vaccination Day
Mon 17	St. Patricks Day
Tue 18	Awkward Moments Day World Social Work Day
Wed 19	National Certified Nurses Day National Chocolate Caramel Day
Thur 20	International Day of Happiness World Oral Health Day
Fri 21	World Down Syndrome Day National Single Parent Day World Poetry Day
Sat 22	World Water Day
Sun 23	National Puppy Day World Meteorological Day
Mon 24	World Tuberculosis Day
Tue 25	National Physician's Week
Wed 26	National Spinach Day
Thur 27	World Theatre Day
Fri 28	Respect Your Cat Day
Sat 29	World Piano Day
Sun 30	UK and Ireland Mother's Day Take a Walk in the Park Day National Doctors' Day
Mon 31	National Crayon Day National Tater Day

Sun	Mon	Tue	Wed	Thu	Fri	Sat
						01
02	03	04	05	06	07	08
09	10	11	12	13	14	15
16	17	18	19	20	21	22
23	24	25	26	27	28	29
30	31					

> Notes

APRIL 2025

Date	Day	Date	Day
Tue 1	April Fool's Day International Fun at Work Day	Wed 16	World Voice Day National Wear Your Pajamas to Work Day
Wed 2	World Autism Awareness Day International Children's Book Day	Thur 17	No Limits For Deaf Children Day
Thur 3	World Party Day National Rainbow Day	Fri 18	International Amateur Radio Day National Columnists Day
Fri 4	International Carrot Day National School Librarian Day	Sat 19	Bicycle Day Husband Appreciation Day
Sat 5	National Handmade Day National Love Our Children Day	Sun 20	Easter Sunday Volunteer Recognition Day
Sun 6	International Day of Sport for Development and Peace International Good Deeds Day	Mon 21	World Creativity and Innovation Day
Mon 7	World Health Day	Tue 22	Earth Day
Tue 8	National Zoo Lovers Day	Wed 23	World Book Night English Language Day
Wed 9	National Unicorn Day	Thur 24	National Skipping Day
Thur 10	National Hug Your Dog Day	Fri 25	World Penguin Day World Malaria Day
Fri 11	National Pet Day World Parkinson's Day	Sat 26	International Chernobyl Disaster Remembrance Day World Intellectual Property Day
Sat 12	National Day of Silence	Sun 27	National Tell A Story Day
Sun 13	National Scrabble Day	Mon 28	National Superhero Day National Great Poetry Reading Day
Mon 14	National Dolphin Day International Moment of Laughter Day	Tue 29	International Dance Day
Tue 15	World Art Day National Laundry Day	Wed 30	International Jazz Day Honesty Day

Sun	Mon	Tue	Wed	Thu	Fri	Sat
		01	02	03	04	05
06	07	08	09	10	11	12
13	14	15	16	17	18	19
20	21	22	23	24	25	26
27	28	29	30			

> Notes

**Claim $377 of free online resources at
www.SellOnSocialMedia.Academy/2025Resources**

MAY 2025

Date	Day
Thur 01	World Password Day
Fri 02	International Harry Potter Day National Brothers and Sisters Day
Sat 03	World Press Freedom Day Astronomy Day
Sun 04	Star Wars Day International Firefighters' Day
Mon 05	National Astronaut Day
Tue 06	International No Diet Day National Nurses Day National Foster Day
Wed 07	Beaufort Scale Day National Tourism Day
Thur 08	World Red Cross and Red Crescent Day National Student Nurse Day
Fri 09	Europe Day
Sat 10	National Clean Your Room Day World Lupus Day World Fair Trade Day
Sun 11	Mothers Day US
Mon 12	International Nurses Day
Tue 13	International Hummus Day
Wed 14	National Receptionists Day
Thurs 15	International Day of Families Peace Officers Memorial Day
Fri 16	National Rollercoaster Day

Date	Day
Sat 17	World Baking Day World Telecommunication and Information Society Day
Sun 18	International Museum Day Emergency Medical Service Day
Mon 19	World Inflammatory Bowel Disease World Family Doctor Day
Tue 20	World Bee Day World Metrology Day
Wed 21	World Day For Cultural Diversity
Thur 22	International Biodiversity Day
Fri 23	World Turtle Day
Sat 24	National Brother's Day
Sun 25	National Wine Day National Missing Children's Day
Mon 26	National Paper Airplane Day Memorial Day
Tue 27	Sunscreen Protection Day
Wed 28	World Blood Cancer Day
Thurs 29	Learn About Composting Day International Day of UN Peacekeepers
Fri 30	World MS Day National Creativity Day
Sat 31	World No Tabacco Day National Smile Day International Flight Attendant Day

Sun	Mon	Tue	Wed	Thu	Fri	Sat
				01	02	03
04	05	06	07	08	09	10
11	12	13	14	15	16	17
18	19	20	21	22	23	24
25	26	27	28	29	30	31

> Notes

 Sell OnSocial.Media

JUNE 2025

Date	Day
Sun 01	National Cancer Survivors Day
Mon 02	National Leave The Office Early Day National Egg Day
Tue 03	World Bicycle Day
Wed 04	National Cognac Day Global Running Day
Thur 05	World Environment Day
Fri 06	National Higher Education Day
Sat 07	World Food Safety Day
Sun 08	World Oceans Day National Best Friend Day
Mon 09	International Archives Day
Tue 10	National Iced Tea Day
Wed 11	World Jaguar Day
Thur 12	World Day Against Child Labour
Fri 13	International Albinism Awareness Day
Sat 14	World Blood Donor Day
Sun 15	Fathers Day World Elder Abuse Awareness Day
Mon 16	Fresh Veggies Day

Date	Day
Tue 17	Eat Your Vegetables Day
Wed 18	International Picnic Day
Thur 19	National Martini Day Juneteenth
Fri 20	World Refugee Day
Sat 21	World Music Day
Sun 22	World Rainforest Day
Mon 23	United Nations Public Service Day
Tue 24	International Fairy Day
Wed 25	Global Beatles Day Day of the Seafarer
Thur 26	National Beautician's Day
Fri 27	National PTSD Awareness Day National Sunglasses Day
Sat 28	National Insurance Awareness Day
Sun 29	National Camera Day
Mon 30	World Social Media Day

Sun	Mon	Tue	Wed	Thu	Fri	Sat
01	02	03	04	05	06	07
08	09	10	11	12	13	14
15	16	17	18	19	20	21
22	23	24	25	26	27	28
29	30					

> Notes

 **Sell OnSocial.Media**

JULY 2025

Date	Day		Date	Day
Tue 1	International Joke Day		Thur 17	World Emoji Day
Wed 2	World UFO Day World Sports Journalists Day		Fri 18	Nelson Mandela International Day
Thur 3	International Plastic Bag Free Day		Sat 19	Daiquiri Day International Karaoke Day
Fri 4	US Independence Day		Sun 20	National Moon Day International Chess Day
Sat 5	National Workaholics Day Pet Remembrance Day		Mon 21	National Junk Food Day
Sun 6	International Kissing Day National Fried Chicken Day		Tue 22	National Hammock Day National Mango Day
Mon 7	World Chocolate Day National Strawberry Sundae Day		Wed 23	National Gorgeous Grandma Day National Vanilla Ice Cream Day
Tue 8	National Video Game Day National Ice Cream Sundae Day		Thur 24	National Tequila Day International Self Care Day
Wed 9	National Sugar Cookie Day Fashion Day		Fri 25	National Wine And Cheese Day
Thur 10	National Pina Colada Day National Kitten Day		Sat 26	National Aunt and Uncle's Day
Fri 11	World Population Day National French Fry Day		Sun 27	Scotch Whisky Day
Sat 12	National Pecan Pie Day		Mon 28	World Nature Conservation Day
Sun 13	International Rock Day		Tue 29	National Lasagne Day International Tiger Day
Mon 14	Bastille Day National Mac & Cheese Day		Wed 30	National Cheesecake Day International Day of Friendship National Father-in-Law Day Paperback Book Day
Tue 15	World Youth Skills Day		Thur 31	National Intern Day National Avocado Day
Wed 16	World Snake Day National Hot Dog Day			

Sun	Mon	Tue	Wed	Thu	Fri	Sat
		01	02	03	04	05
06	07	08	09	10	11	12
13	14	15	16	17	18	19
20	21	22	23	24	25	26
27	28	29	30	31		

> Notes

 Sell OnSocial.Media

AUGUST 2025

Date	Day		Date	Day
Fri 01	International Beer Day Respect For Parents Day National Girlfriend Day		Sat 16	National Rollercoaster Day National Tell A Joke Day World Honey Bee Day
Sat 02	National Colouring Book Day National Ice Cream Sandwich Day		Sun 17	National Thrift Shop Day National Black Cat Appreciation Day
Sun 03	National Sisters Day National Watermelon Day		Mon 18	National Fajita Day National Couples Day
Mon 04	Assistance Dog Day National White Wine Day National Chocolate Chip Cookie Day		Tue 19	World Photography Day
Tue 05	National Oyster Day Blogger Day		Wed 20	National Finance Brokers Day National Radio Day World Mosquito Day
Wed 06	National Fresh Breathe Day Farmworker Appreciation Day		Thur 21	Internet Self-Care Day National Senior Citizens Day
Thur 07	National Lighthouse Day		Fri 22	National Eat a Peach Day
Fri 08	International Cat Day		Sat 23	Health Unit Coordinators Day
Sat 09	National Book Lovers Day		Sun 24	National Waffles Day
Sun 10	National Lazy Day International Vlogging Day National Spoil Your Dog Day		Mon 25	National Whiskey Sour Day National Banana Split Day
Mon 11	National Son and Daughter Day		Tue 26	National Dog Day Women's Equality Day
Tue 12	World Elephant Day International Youth Day		Wed 27	Crab Soup Day
Wed 13	National Prosecco Day International Lefthanders Day		Thur 28	National Red Wine Day
Thur 14	National Social Security Day		Fri 29	National Chop Suey Day National Lemon Juice Day
Fri 15	National Relaxation Day World Greatness Day		Sat 30	International Whale Shark Day National Beach Day
			Sun 31	We Love Memoirs Day World Distance Learning Day

Sun	Mon	Tue	Wed	Thu	Fri	Sat
					01	02
03	04	05	06	07	08	09
10	11	12	13	14	15	16
17	18	19	20	21	22	23
24	25	26	27	28	29	30
31						

> Notes

SEPTEMBER 2025

Date	Day
Mon 01	International Coffee Day Ginger Cat Appreciation Day World Letter Writing Day US Labour Day
Tue 02	World Coconut Day
Wed 03	National Skyscraper Day
Thur 04	National Macadamia Nut Day
Fri 05	International Day of Charity
Sat 06	National Read a Book Day
Sun 07	National Salami Day National Grandparents Day
Mon 08	World Physical Therapy Day
Tue 09	International Sudoku Day
Wed 10	World Suicide Prevention Day
Thur 11	National Hot Cross Bun Day
Fri 12	National Video Games Day Stand Up To Cancer Day
Sat 13	International Chocolate Day
Sun 14	National Cream Filled Donut Day
Mon 15	Greenpeace Day
Tue 16	Working Parents Day World Barber Day
Wed 17	International Country Music Day National Pet Bird Day

Date	Day
Thur 18	International Read an eBook Day
Fri 19	National Tradesman Day
Sat 20	National Dance Day
Sun 21	International Day of Peace World Gratitude Day World Alzheimer's Day
Mon 22	Business Womens Day National Family Day World Rhino Day
Tue 23	International Day of Sign Languages
Wed 24	National Punctuation Day
Thur 25	National Daughters Day World Pharmacists Day World Maritime Day
Fri 26	National Baker Day HR Professional Day Save The Koala Day
Sat 27	National Chocolate Milk Day World Tourism Day International Lace Day
Sun 28	World River Day
Mon 29	International Day of Food Waste Awareness World Heart Day
Tue 30	International Podcast Day

Sun	Mon	Tue	Wed	Thu	Fri	Sat
	01	02	03	04	05	06
07	08	09	10	11	12	13
14	15	16	17	18	19	20
21	22	23	24	25	26	27
28	29	30				

> Notes

 **Sell OnSocial.Media**

OCTOBER 2025

Date	Day
Wed 01	International Coffee Day World Vegetarian Day International Music Day World Financial Planning Day
Thur 02	International Day of Non-Violence National Poetry Day
Fri 03	World Boyfriend Day World Smile Day
Sat 04	National Golf Lovers Day World Animal Day
Sun 05	World Teachers Day
Mon 06	World Architecture Day National Physician Assistant Day
Tue 07	World Cotton Day
Wed 08	World Octopus Day National Emergency Nurses Day
Thur 09	World Post Day Fire Prevention Day
Fri 10	World Mental Health Day World Homeless Day World Egg Day
Sat 11	International Day of the Girl Child World Hospice and Palliative Care Day
Sun 12	World Arthritis Day
Mon 13	International Day for Disaster Risk Reduction Canadian Thanksgiving Columbus Day
Tue 14	National Dessert Day

Date	Day
Wed 15	World Students Day
Thur 16	World Food Day
Fri 17	International Day for the Eradication of Poverty National Pasta Day
Sat 18	World Menopause Day
Sun 19	International Gin & Tonic Day
Mon 20	International Chefs Day International Sloth Day
Tue 21	National Apple Day
Wed 22	National Nut Day International Stuttering Awareness Day
Thur 23	International Snow Leopard Day National Paralegal Day
Fri 24	United Nations Day
Sat 25	World Pasta Day International Artist Day National Make a Difference Day
Sun 26	National Microneedling Day National Mother-in-Law Day
Mon 27	National Mentoring Day
Tue 28	National First Responders Day
Wed 29	World Stroke Day
Thur 30	National Candy Corn Day
Fri 31	National Magic Day Halloween

Sun	Mon	Tue	Wed	Thu	Fri	Sat
			01	02	03	04
05	06	07	08	09	10	11
12	13	14	15	16	17	18
19	20	21	22	23	24	25
26	27	28	29	30	31	

> Notes

 Sell OnSocial.Media

NOVEMBER 2025

Date	Day	Date	Day
Sat 01	World Vegan Day All Saints' Day National Adoption Month	Sun 16	National Fast Food Day
Sun 02	International Day to End Impunity for Crimes Against Journalists	Mon 17	National Homemade Bread Day
		Tue 18	Mickey Mouse Day
Mon 03	National Sandwich Day	Wed 19	International Mens Day Entrepreneurs Day
Tue 04	National Candy Day	Thur 20	World Childrens Day
Wed 05	National Love Your Red Hair Day National Stress Awareness Day	Fri 21	World Television Day
Thur 06	National Nachos Day	Sat 22	Go For a Ride Day
Fri 07	National Hug a Bear Day	Sun 23	National Espresso Day
Sat 08	National Cappuccino Day	Mon 24	National Sardines Day
Sun 09	World Freedom Day	Tue 25	National Parfait Day
Mon 10	National Vanilla Cupcake Day	Wed 26	National Cake Day
Tue 11	Singles Day, Veterans Day	Thur 27	Thanksgiving Turtle Adoption Day
Wed 12	World Pneumonia Day	Fri 28	National French Toast Day Black Friday
Thur 13	World Kindness Day	Sat 29	Small Business Saturday
Fri 14	World Diabetes Day	Sun 30	Remembrance Day for Lost Species
Sat 15	National Recycling Day		

Sun	Mon	Tue	Wed	Thu	Fri	Sat
						01
02	03	04	05	06	07	08
09	10	11	12	13	14	15
16	17	18	19	20	21	22
23	24	25	26	27	28	29
30						

> Notes

 Sell OnSocial.Media

DECEMBER 2025

Date	Day
Mon 01	Cyber Monday National Christmas Lights Day
Tue 02	National Mutt Day
Wed 03	International Day of Persons with Disabilities
Thur 04	National Cookie Day
Fri 05	International Soil Day
Sat 06	St. Nicholas Day
Sun 07	National Cotton Candy Day
Mon 08	National Brownie Day
Tue 09	Anti-Corruption Day
Wed 10	International Human Rights Day
Thur 11	International Mountain Day
Fri 12	Gingerbread House Day
Sat 13	National Cocoa Day
Sun 14	Monkey Day
Mon 15	National Cupcake Day
Tue 16	National Chocolate Covered Anything Day

Date	Day
Wed 17	National Maple Syrup Day
Thur 18	International Migrants Day
Fri 19	National Hard Candy Day National Ugly Sweater Day
Sat 20	International Human Solidarity Day
Sun 21	National Short Story Day
Mon 22	National Cookies Exchange Day
Tue 23	National Roots Day
Wed 24	National Eggnog Day
Thur 25	Christmas Day
Fri 26	National Candy Cane Day Boxing Day
Sat 27	Visit The Zoo Day
Sun 28	National Call a Friend Day
Mon 29	Tick Tock Day
Tue 30	National Bacon Day
Wed 31	New Years Eve National Champagne Day

Sun	Mon	Tue	Wed	Thu	Fri	Sat
	01	02	03	04	05	06
07	08	09	10	11	12	13
14	15	16	17	18	19	20
21	22	23	24	25	26	27
28	29	30	31			

> Notes

JANUARY 2025
WEEK 1

> **Monday 30 December**

> **Tuesday 31**

> **Wednesday 01 January**

IRE, UK, US - New Year's Day

> TO DO THIS WEEK

> Thursday 02

> Friday 03

> Saturday 04

> Sunday 05

JANUARY 2025
WEEK 2

> Monday 06

> Tuesday 07

> Wednesday 08

> TO DO THIS WEEK

> **Thursday 09**

> **Friday 10**

> **Saturday 11**

> **Sunday 12**

JANUARY 2025

WEEK 3

> Monday 13

> Tuesday 14

> Wednesday 15

> Thursday 16

> Friday 17

> Saturday 18

> Sunday 19

JANUARY 2025
WEEK 4

> Monday 20

US - Martin Luther King Jr. Day

> Tuesday 21

> Wednesday 22

> TO DO THIS WEEK

> Thursday 23

> Friday 24

> Saturday 25

> Sunday 26

JANUARY / FEBRUARY 2025
WEEK 5

> Monday 27

> Tuesday 28

> Wednesday 29

> TO DO THIS WEEK

> Thursday 30

> Friday 31

> Saturday 01 February

> Sunday 02

FEBRUARY 2025
WEEK 6

> ### Monday 03

IRE - Bank Holiday

> ### Tuesday 04

> ### Wednesday 05

> TO DO THIS WEEK

> Thursday 06

> Friday 07

> Saturday 08

> Sunday 09

**Sell OnSocial.Media**

> Monday 10

> Tuesday 11

> Wednesday 12

> TO DO THIS WEEK

> Thursday 13

> Friday 14

> Saturday 15

> Sunday 16

FEBRUARY 2025
WEEK 8

> **Monday 17**

US - President's Day

> **Tuesday 18**

> **Wednesday 19**

> Thursday 20

> Friday 21

> Saturday 22

> Sunday 23

FEBRUARY / MARCH 2025
WEEK 9

> Monday 24

> Tuesday 25

> Wednesday 26

> Thursday 27

> Friday 28

> Saturday 01 March

> Sunday 02

Sell OnSocial.Media

MARCH 2025
WEEK 10

> Monday 03

> Tuesday 04

> Wednesday 05

> TO DO THIS WEEK

> Thursday 06

> Friday 07

> Saturday 08

> Sunday 09

MARCH 2025
WEEK 11

> Monday 10

> Tuesday 11

> Wednesday 12

> **Thursday 13**

> **Friday 14**

> Saturday 15

> Sunday 16

MARCH 2025
WEEK 12

> **Monday 17**

IRE - Bank Holiday

> **Tuesday 18**

> **Wednesday 19**

> TO DO THIS WEEK

> Thursday 20

> Friday 21

> Saturday 22

> Sunday 23

MARCH 2025
WEEK 13

> ### Monday 24

> ### Tuesday 25

> ### Wednesday 26

> TO DO THIS WEEK

> Thursday 27

> Friday 28

> Saturday 29

> Sunday 30

MARCH / APRIL 2025
WEEK 14

> Monday 31

> Tuesday 01 April

> Wednesday 02

> TO DO THIS WEEK

> **Thursday 03**

> **Friday 04**

> Saturday 05

> Sunday 06

APRIL 2025
WEEK 15

> Monday 07

> Tuesday 08

> Wednesday 09

> Thursday 10

> Friday 11

> Saturday 12

> Sunday 13

APRIL 2025
WEEK 16

> Monday 14

> Tuesday 15

> Wednesday 16

> TO DO THIS WEEK

> Thursday 17

> Friday 18

UK - Good Friday

> Saturday 19

> Sunday 20

APRIL 2025
WEEK 17

> **Monday 21**

IRE, UK - Bank Holiday

> **Tuesday 22**

> **Wednesday 23**

> TO DO THIS WEEK

> Thursday 24

> Friday 25

> Saturday 26

> Sunday 27

APRIL / MAY 2025
WEEK 18

> Monday 28

> Tuesday 29

> Wednesday 30

> TO DO THIS WEEK

> Thursday 01 May

> Friday 02

> Saturday 03

> Sunday 04

MAY 2025
WEEK 19

> Monday 05

IRE, UK - Bank Holiday

> Tuesday 06

> Wednesday 07

> TO DO THIS WEEK

> Thursday 08

> Friday 09

> Saturday 10

> Sunday 11

MAY 2025
WEEK 20

> Monday 12

> Tuesday 13

> Wednesday 14

> Thursday 15

> Friday 16

> Saturday 17

> Sunday 18

MAY 2025
WEEK 21

> Monday 19

> Tuesday 20

> Wednesday 21

> TO DO THIS WEEK

> Thursday 22

> Friday 23

> Saturday 24

> Sunday 25

MAY / JUNE 2025
WEEK 22

> ### Monday 26

UK - Bank Holiday / US - Memorial Day

> ### Tuesday 27

> ### Wednesday 28

> Thursday 29

> Friday 30

> Saturday 31

> Sunday 01 June

JUNE 2025
WEEK 23

> ### Monday 02

IRE - Bank Holiday

> ### Tuesday 03

> ### Wednesday 04

> TO DO THIS WEEK

> Thursday 05

> Friday 06

> Saturday 07

> Sunday 08

JUNE 2025
WEEK 24

> Monday 09

> Tuesday 10

> Wednesday 11

> TO DO THIS WEEK

> Thursday 12

> Friday 13

> Saturday 14

> Sunday 15

JUNE 2025
WEEK 25

> Monday 16

> Tuesday 17

> Wednesday 18

> TO DO THIS WEEK

> Thursday 19

> Friday 20

> Saturday 21

> Sunday 22

JUNE 2025
WEEK 26

> Monday 23

> Tuesday 24

> Wednesday 25

> Thursday 26

> Friday 27

> Saturday 28

> Sunday 29

JUNE / JULY 2025
WEEK 27

> Monday 30

> Tuesday 01 July

> Wednesday 02

> TO DO THIS WEEK

> Thursday 03

> Friday 04

US - Independence Day

> Saturday 05

> Sunday 06

JULY 2025
WEEK 28

> Monday 07

> Tuesday 08

> Wednesday 09

> Thursday 10

> Friday 11

> Saturday 12

> Sunday 13

JULY 2025
WEEK 29

> **Monday 14**

> **Tuesday 15**

> **Wednesday 16**

> TO DO THIS WEEK

> Thursday 17

> Friday 18

> Saturday 19

> Sunday 20

JULY 2025
WEEK 30

> Monday 21

> Tuesday 22

> Wednesday 23

> TO DO THIS WEEK

> Thursday 24

> Friday 25

> Saturday 26

> Sunday 27

JULY / AUGUST 2025
WEEK 31

> Monday 28

> Tuesday 29

> Wednesday 30

> TO DO THIS WEEK

> Thursday 31

> Friday 01 August

> Saturday 02

> Sunday 03

Sell OnSocial.Media

AUGUST 2025
WEEK 32

> **Monday 04**

IRE - August Bank Holiday

> **Tuesday 05**

> **Wednesday 06**

> **Thursday 07**

> **Friday 08**

> Saturday 09

> Sunday 10

AUGUST 2025
WEEK 33

> Monday 11

> Tuesday 12

> Wednesday 13

> Thursday 14

> Friday 15

> Saturday 16

> Sunday 17

AUGUST 2025
WEEK 34

> Monday 18

> Tuesday 19

> Wednesday 20

> TO DO THIS WEEK

> Thursday 21

> Friday 22

> Saturday 23

> Sunday 24

AUGUST 2025
WEEK 35

> **Monday 25 August**

UK - Bank Holiday

> **Tuesday 26**

> **Wednesday 27**

> Thursday 28

> Friday 29

> Saturday 30

> Sunday 31

SEPTEMBER 2025
WEEK 36

> Monday 01

US - Labor Day

> Tuesday 02

> Wednesday 03

> Thursday 04

> Friday 05

> Saturday 06

> Sunday 07

SEPTEMBER 2025
WEEK 37

> Monday 08

> Tuesday 09

> Wednesday 10

> **Thursday 11**

> **Friday 12**

> Saturday 13

> Sunday 14

SEPTEMBER 2025
WEEK 38

> **Monday 15**

> **Tuesday 16**

> **Wednesday 17**

> Thursday 18

> Friday 19

> Saturday 20

> Sunday 21

SEPTEMBER 2025
WEEK 39

> Monday 22

> Tuesday 23

> Wednesday 24

> TO DO THIS WEEK

> Thursday 25

> Friday 26

> Saturday 27

> Sunday 28

SEPTEMBER / OCTOBER 2025
WEEK 40

> Monday 29

> Tuesday 30

> Wednesday 01 October

> TO DO THIS WEEK

> Thursday 02

> Friday 03

> Saturday 04

> Sunday 05

Sell OnSocial.Media

OCTOBER 2025
WEEK 41

> Monday 06

> Tuesday 07

> Wednesday 08

> TO DO THIS WEEK

> Thursday 09

> Friday 10

> Saturday 11

> Sunday 12

OCTOBER 2025
WEEK 42

> Monday 13

> Tuesday 14

> Wednesday 15

> Thursday 16

> Friday 17

> Saturday 18

> Sunday 19

OCTOBER 2025
WEEK 43

> Monday 20

> Tuesday 21

> Wednesday 22

> TO DO THIS WEEK

> Thursday 23

> Friday 24

> Saturday 25

> Sunday 26

OCTOBER / NOVEMBER 2025
WEEK 44

> **Monday 27**

IRE - Bank Holiday

> **Tuesday 28**

> **Wednesday 29**

> **Thursday 30**

> **Friday 31**

> **Saturday 01 November**

> **Sunday 02**

NOVEMBER 2025
WEEK 45

> **Monday 03**

> **Tuesday 04**

> **Wednesday 05**

> TO DO THIS WEEK

> Thursday 06

> Friday 07

> Saturday 08

> Sunday 09

NOVEMBER 2025
WEEK 46

> Monday 10

> Tuesday 11

US - Veterans Day

> Wednesday 12

> TO DO THIS WEEK

> Thursday 13

> Friday 14

> Saturday 15

> Sunday 16

NOVEMBER 2025
WEEK 47

> Monday 17

> Tuesday 18

> Wednesday 19

> **Thursday 20**

> **Friday 21**

> Saturday 22

> Sunday 23

NOVEMBER 2025
WEEK 48

> Monday 24

> Tuesday 25

> Wednesday 26

> Thursday 27

US - Thanksgiving

> Friday 28

> Saturday 29

> Sunday 30

DECEMBER 2025
WEEK 49

> Monday 01

> Tuesday 02

> Wednesday 03

> TO DO THIS WEEK

> Thursday 04

> Friday 05

> Saturday 06

> Sunday 07

DECEMBER 2025
WEEK 50

> Monday 08

> Tuesday 09

> Wednesday 10

> **Thursday 11**

> **Friday 12**

> **Saturday 13**

> **Sunday 14**

DECEMBER 2025
WEEK 51

> Monday 15

> Tuesday 16

> Wednesday 17

> TO DO THIS WEEK

> Thursday 18

> Friday 19

> Saturday 20

> Sunday 21

DECEMBER 2025
WEEK 52

> Monday 22

> Tuesday 23

> Wednesday 24

> TO DO THIS WEEK

> Thursday 25

IRE - Christmas Day / UK - Christmas Day / US - Christmas Day

> Friday 26

IRE - St Stephen's Day / UK - Boxing Day

> Saturday 27

> Sunday 28

DECEMBER 2025 / JANUARY 2026
WEEK 1

> Monday 29

> Tuesday 30

> Wednesday 31

> TO DO THIS WEEK

> Thursday 01 January 2026

New Years Day

> Friday 02

> Saturday 03

> Sunday 04